PORPHYRY'S LETTER TO HIS WIFE MARCELLA

Porphyry's Letter to His Wife Marcella

CONCERNING THE LIFE OF PHILOSOPHY AND THE ASCENT TO THE GODS

TRANSLATED FROM THE GREEK BY
ALICE ZIMMERN

WITH AN INTRODUCTION BY
DAVID R. FIDELER

PHANES PRESS
GRAND RAPIDS
1986

Alice Zimmern's translation first appeared in *Porphyry the Philosopher to His Wife Marcella*, published by George Redway, London, 1896. The translation has been totally reset and is identical with the original, with the exception that the archaic forms of the personal pronoun have been modernized in this edition.

Published by Phanes Press, PO Box 6114, Grand Rapids, Michigan 49506, U.S.A.

Typography by Archetype Graphics, Grand Rapids, Michigan. The text was set in Goudy Oldstyle on Compugraphic photocomposition equipment.

Library of Congress Cataloging-in-Publication Data

Porphyry, ca. 234-ca. 305.
   Porphyry's letter to his wife Marcella.

   Translation of: Pros Markellan.
   Bibliography: p.
   1. Ethics, Ancient. 2. God—Early works to 1800.
3. Markella. I. Markella. II. Zimmern, Alice, 1855-1939.
III. Fideler, David R., date. IV. Title.
B697.P742E5 1986   171'.3   85-29718
ISBN 0-933999-27-5 (alk. paper)

This book is printed on alkaline paper which conforms to the permanent paper standard developed by the National Information Standards Organization.

Contents

Introduction by David Fideler

The Letter to Marcella

INTRODUCTION

Porphyry: His Life and Work

WRITING OF PORPHYRY the philosopher, his biographer Eunapius of Sardis rightly observed that "one may well be at a loss and wonder within oneself which branch [of knowledge] he studied more than another... As for philosophy, I cannot describe in words his genius for discourse, or for moral philosophy."[1]

Of his life a few biographical details are known.

Porphyry was born in Tyre, the capital of Phoenicia, around 233 of the common era. Being a port city and the leading center for the manufacture of Tyrian purple dye, Tyre boasted an active economy and was a nexus point of international trade. It was here that Porphyry as a young man had the opportunity to study a variety of languages, cultures and religious beliefs. While Porphyry was of Semitic descent and his native tongue was Syriac, he was educated in Greek and became a true master of that language.

While still a young man Porphyry had the opportunity to hear Origen, the great Christian intellectual, lecturing in Caesarea. But Porphyry found Origen's attempt to reconcile Christianity with the Greek intellectual tradition to be profoundly absurd, and he would note later in life that Origen, while being "a Greek schooled in Greek thought, plunged headlong into un-Greek recklessness;

immersed in this, he peddled himself and his skill in argument. In his way of life he behaved like a Christian... in his metaphysical and theological ideas he played the Greek, giving a Greek twist to foreign tales."[2] It seemed to Porphyry, and perhaps justifiably, that Origen's attempted synthesis of Platonic metaphysics and Christian revelation was an exercise in intellectual sophistry and, more seriously, a betrayal of Greek philosophy and the principles of intellectual inquiry.

In his early twenties Porphyry went to Athens where he studied under the rhetorician and philosopher Longinus, a man whom Eunapius characterized as "a living library and walking museum."[3] It was Longinus who bestowed the name of 'Porphyry' on the young scholar. In Syriac his name was Malchus, which means king, and Longinus suggested that he adopt Porphyry, the Greek name for purple, the regal color.

In the intellectual atmosphere of Athens Porphyry's initial studies flourished, and it may have been under Longinus that he had his first real exposure to the profundities of Platonic thought.[4] Yet while Porphyry may well have been exposed to the Platonic (and Pythagorean) tradition at this time, he appears to have busied himself mainly with literary criticism and textual scholarship. For this he could not have had a better teacher, and it was in Athens that he published his first work of literary criticism, the *Homeric Questions*. Under Longinus Porphyry firmly mastered the scholarly skills of literary, textual and historical criticism which he would later employ in his analyses of Christian scriptures; and it was under the beneficent tutelage of Longinus that Porphyry's rhetorical clarity and prowess, which is unmistakably evidenced in all his writing, was guided to complete fruition. Indeed, it is precisely this clarity of expression which led Eunapius to liken our philosopher to "a chain of Hermes let down to mortals."[5]

Porphyry studied in Athens with Longinus for a period of several years. During this period he absorbed as much as he possibly could and, one is tempted to speculate, as much as there possibly was to absorb. But on hearing of Plotinus's teachings, Porphyry knew that he must go to Rome. This was in the year 263 when Porphyry was 30 years old and Plotinus was about 60.

* * *

Like Porphyry, Plotinus had once been a restless student. He attended the lectures of various philosophers in Alexandria but always left with a feeling of dissatisfaction, a feeling of incompleteness. Relating his feelings of sadness and depression to one of his friends, Plotinus was instructed to attend a lecture of a certain Ammonius, a self-taught philosopher. Having attended the lecture, Plotinus returned to his friend and stated succinctly, "This is the man I was looking for." Plotinus was to spend the next 11 years of his life studying with Ammonius.

There can be no doubt that when Porphyry arrived in Rome he discovered in Plotinus 'the man he had been looking for.' What we know of Plotinus's life and character we learn from Porphyry's biography of the man. Porphyry, who gives a typically thorough account, tells us that assembled around Plotinus in Rome was a circle of students and admirers including Roman senators, physicians, and other distinguished hearers of both sexes. Even the Emperor and his wife "honoured and venerated" Plotinus, who certainly had an extensive and unique following for a metaphysical philosopher. Porphyry quickly became his closest friend and was eventually entrusted with the task of editing the writings of Plotinus, which Porphyry grouped into six groups of nine (*ennea*), and which thus became known as the *Enneads*.

In Porphyry's biography many interesting details about Plotinus and his circle are related, and some interesting autobiographical details are reported as well. For example, Porphyry tells us that when he first arrived in Rome he wrote a treatise against Plotinus in order to demonstrate that the objects of thought exist outside the intellect. Plotinus had Amelius, a long-time student, read Porphyry's essay to him. After hearing the piece Plotinus smiled and said, "You shall have the task of solving thse difficulties, Amelius. He has fallen into them because he does not know what we hold." As Porphyry recalls,

> Amelius wrote a lengthy treatise "In Answer to Porphyry's Difficulties"; I replied to what he had written; Amelius answered my reply; and the third time with difficulty I understood the doctrine, changed my mind and wrote a recantation which I read in the meeting of the school. After this I believed in Plotinus's writings, and tried to rouse in the master himself the ambition to organise his doctrine and write it down more at length; and I also stimulated Amelius's desire to write books.[6]

Porphyry also tells of the time that he recited an allegorical poem on *The Sacred Marriage* at a feast of Plato, an annual banquet traditionally celebrated by Platonists.

However, "because much in it was expressed in the mysterious and veiled language of inspiration someone said, 'Porphyry is mad.' But Plotinus said, so as to be heard by all, 'You have shown yourself at once poet, philosopher, and expounder of sacred mysteries.' "[7]

For similar anecdotes the reader is refered to Porphyry's interesting and unusual *Life of Plotinus* which accompanies most editions of the *Enneads*.

Porphyry studied with Plotinus for six years until he came under the spell of *melancholia* and even contemplated the possibility of suicide. But Plotinus, who "had a surpassing degree of penetration into character," noticed that not all was well with Porphyry, and suggested that a little travel might do him well. Following Plotinus's suggestion he set off for Sicily. Unfortunately, Plotinus died in 270 while Porphyry was away.

Porphyry remained active while in Sicily. It was there that he worked on the problems of Aristotelian logic, composing his *Isagoge* (or Introduction) to the five categories of Aristotle. This work, written for the Roman Senator Chrysaorius, seeks to explain the five Aristotelian predicables of genus, species, difference, property and accident to the beginning student.[8] Porphyry also wrote other works while in Sicily, including a simple commentary on the categories of Arisotle, a work comparing the thought of Plato and Aristotle, as well as his massive polemic *Against the Christians*, which was later sentenced to be burned by the Council of Ephesus (431) and by a law of Theodosius II (448), and is consequently difficult to study since only questionable fragments remain.

Porphyry was in fact a prolific writer, producing commentaries on the writings of the great philosophers, and treating such topics as history and biography, metaphysics, psychology, ethics, the philosophical interpretation of myths, rhetoric and grammar, mathematics, astronomy and musical harmonics. While many of his writings have perished, among those which survive are:

• *The Life of Pythagoras* (from his longer *History of Philosophy*)

• His *Life of Plotinus*

• *Launching-Points to the Realm of Mind* (otherwise known as the *Auxiliaries to the Perception of Intelligible Natures*)

• His *Treatise on the Five Predicables* (i.e., the *Isagoge*)

• *On the Cave of the Nymphs*

• A *Commentary on the Harmonics of Ptolemy*

• An *Epistle to Anebo the Egyptian* (on the topic of theurgy)

• *On Abstinence from Animal Food*

• The *Homeric Questions*

• Excerpts from *Concerning the Soul*

• Porphyry's *Letter to Marcella*

• And numerous fragments

In sum, the known titles of the Porphyrian corpus exceeds 75 in number, and a complete list is given as an appendix to the Phanes edition of the *Launching-Points to the Realm of Mind*. One can only conclude that the wide range of learning which Porphyry exhibited in his books and tractates firmly secures his position as one of the great figures of the Western intellectual tradition; in fact, so radiant was his reputation that even Porphyry's arch-critic St. Augustine could not help but refer to him as "the most learned of the philosophers."

After the death of his master Plotinus, Porphyry returned to Rome to assume leadership of the school, and it was around 298 that Porphyry published the *Enneads* and his *Life of Plotinus*. Shortly after the year 300, as he approached the age of 70, Porphyry married Marcella for the reasons described in his *Letter*. He is thought to have died, probably in Rome, between 302 and 306 of the common era.

Porphyry, Christianity, and Neoplatonism

If one were to remove the few passing references to the 'gods' in the *Letter to Marcella*, and place Porphyry's work in the hands of an unsuspecting reader, that reader might easily take the work to be an exposition of the highest Christian moral philosophy. Yet, if Neoplatonism and early Christianity are indistinguishable in terms of the high ethical standards that they both espouse, what was it that compelled Porphyry to write *Against the Christians*? And exactly how is it that Christianity differs from Neoplatonism? While we cannot answer these questions fully in the space available, it is nonetheless possible to briefly illuminate some of the issues involved.

Porphyry wrote two major works which relate to Christianity. *Against the Christians* is said to have consisted of 15 books and mostly dealt with historical and textual criticism of the four gospels and other writings, such as the "Book of Daniel," which were often quoted by the early Christians to justify their beliefs. Porphyry was in fact the first scholar to apply the canons of historical criticism to the books of the Bible, and he was the first to correctly point out that the "Book of Daniel" could not have been written until the reign of Antiochus Ephiphanes, thus showing that the events referred to in the 'prophecies' had actually occurred *before* the book was written.[9] In this work Porphyry also exposed the many inconsistencies which exist between the gospel narratives, thus showing that they cannot be regarded as accurate historical accounts.

The other work in which Porphyry alluded to Christianity was called *The Philosophy from Oracles*, "a description and compilation of responses, ostensibly divine, on matters of philosophical interest."[10] In this work Porphyry attempted to demonstrate the relationship which existed between the popular religious beliefs and practices of various nations and the views of philosophers concerning the nature of God and the gods.

To the Neoplatonist the universe consists of the outpouring of one divine life which manifests itself on different levels of reality, 'descending' in a hierarchical fashion. At the summit of this divine hierarchy is the one supreme God, and subordinate to This are the lesser gods who have their source in the One. The gods exist, to be sure, but like all beings they depend strictly on their source. As Plotinus observes concerning this 'polytheistic' perspective, "It is not contracting the divine into one but showing it in that multiplicity in which God himself has shown it which is proper to those who know the power of God, inasmuch as, abiding who he is, he makes many gods, all depending upon himself and existing through him and from him."[11]

Porphyry's *Philosophy from Oracles* was divided into three parts, each part treating one level of the celestial hierarchy. Hence, the first book dealt with the one supreme God and the subordinate Olympian deities; book two was about the daimones or celestial intelligences; and the third book discussed the souls of the divine heroes such as Orpheus, Pythagoras, and Heracles. In the course of his presentation Porphyry quoted certain divine oracles, and a number of those which relate to Christianity have been preserved by Saint Augustine in his *City of God.*

What did the gods have to say about Jesus and the Christians?

Porphyry notes that what he has to say "may appear startling to some" and then goes on to note that "the gods have pronounced Christ to have been extremely devout, and they have said that he has become immortal, and that they mention him in terms of commendation." However, concerning the Christians, the gods have said that they are "polluted and contaminated and entangled in error."[12] Throughout the oracles quoted by Porphyry the gods speak highly of Jesus, noting that he was a great spiritual teacher who instructed his followers to worship God the Father. Why is it, then, that the goddess Hecate, in an oracle quoted by Porphyry, states that 'You should not speak ill of Christ, but pity the folly of mankind'?

The answer to this lies in the fact that while Jesus directed the minds of men to contemplate the nature of the one high God, the *followers* of Jesus instructed men to worship Jesus instead of God. It was from this perspective that another oracle of Hecate states that Jesus "was a most devout man, and that his soul, like the souls of other devout men, was endowed after death with the immortality it deserved" but went on to say with disapproval "that Christians in their ignorance worship this soul."

When Porphyry speaks of Jesus it is always with respect. But his attitude toward Christianity could only be critical, for in his view it was "an irrational and unexamined faith," which is to say a system of false opinion, that was leading men to turn away from God by identifying Jesus with the supreme principle. To Porphyry this was blasphemous, impious and lawless for, by turning men and women away from the worship of the supreme principle, it undercut the traditional piety that was such an important foundation stone of classical civilization. Porphyry never did suggest that persecution of the Christians was a satisfactory solution to the dilemma, for as a philosopher he clearly recognized that the evil characteristic of unreasoning belief could not be eliminated by the unintelligible evil characteristic of brute force. Rather, as E.R. Dodds noted, Porphyry "seems to have spoken with pity of the many Christians whom the teaching of their church has caused 'to be inhumanely punished.' "[13]

Robert Wilken, who has done much to clearly elucidate Porphyry's attitude toward Christianity, observes in his book *The Christians as the Romans Saw Them* that

> Christians feared Porphyry's *Philosophy from Oracles* because it was the first work to give a positive appraisal of Jesus within the framework of pagan religion. Precisely at the time Porphyry was writing his book, Christian leaders were on the verge of a major dispute about the status of Christ... Was Jesus to be thought of as fully God, equal to the one high God? Or was he a lesser deity, who, though sharing an intimate relation to God the Father, was nevertheless second in rank? To place Jesus among the Greek heroes was, in the minds of the pagans,

to give him a lofty place indeed, for this put him in a class with Heracles or Pythagoras. But to those Christians who were beginning to claim that Jesus was equal to the one high God, it was a stinging rebuttal.[14]

* * *

According to Platonic epistemology, the cognitive states of knowledge and belief relate to separate levels of being. While opinion may be either true or false, and while true opinion may lead to the same pragmatic result as actual knowledge, there must nonetheless remain a major epistemological difference between knowledge and opinion. Porphyry referred to Christianity as an 'unreasoning faith,' and earlier the Greek physician Galen had observed that while Christians appeared to exhibit the virtues of courage, temperance and justice, they lacked intellectual insight, the proper basis of the other three. Likewise, the Emperor Julian would protest that "There is nothing in your philosophy beyond the one word 'Believe'!"[15]

Porphyry writes in the *Letter to Marcella* that "There are four first principles that must be upheld concerning God—faith, truth, love, hope. We must have faith that our only salvation is in turning to God. And having faith, we must strive with all our might to know the truth about God. And when we know this, we must love Him we do know. And when we love Him we must nourish our souls on good hopes for our life, for it is by their good hopes good men are superior to bad ones."[16] The faith of which Porphyry speaks, as J.M. Rist has shown, is not that of the unreasoning variety (to which Porphyry refers earlier), but rather represents the firm, rational confidence that an individual's salvation lies in returning to his source.[17] Note also that such faith leads to knowledge of God rather that to mere belief.

To the Neoplatonist the soul is by its very nature a divine entity. Because the soul has its origin in the world of eternal principles, it is by turning to these principles and becoming cognizant of them that the soul realizes its salvation, its own inherent immortality. Hence there is no need for the saving grace of an external agency, for the soul already contains within it its own potential salvation. This recognition of the soul's source and nature is, according to the Neoplatonists, a rational one, based on an intelligible realization of the way things are, an awakening to the ontological level. At this level faith must be inferior to knowledge: indeed, it is in an altogether different class, for mere opinion or belief cannot effect the realization of the way things are, the knowledge of eternal being. Porphyry saw that *Christianity taught that mere belief is enough to insure one's salvation*—and thus he saw within Christianity a decidedly anti-intellectual tendency, dangerous to the cultivation of the soul, its true spiritual development, and the ongoing process of philosophical inquiry.

In its detailed approach to the nature of the philosophical ascent to God, Neoplatonism may be justifiably seen as the preeminent mystical philosophy of the West. Yet, while God or the One is the source of all—and must then necessarily exist beyond and above the realm of Intellect—there is never any conflict between 'mysticism' and 'rationality' in Neoplatonism for *it is only through the use of the intellect that the One may be reached.* To quote Plotinus, "There are no shortcuts." Indeed, as A.H. Armstrong has observed, "for Plotinus there is no way of passing beyond intellect other than through intellect. We cannot leave our philosophical minds behind till we have used them to the full. There is, in his way of thinking, no alternative route to God for non-philosophers."[18]

It is true that the influence of 'Neoplatonic' thought on the development of the later Christian mystical tradition cannot be overstressed. Yet the Christian form of the mystical ascent severed its connection with Plotinian Neoplatonism in as far as it neglected to teach that the One may be reached only by first passing through the realm of Mind.

Some Characteristics of Neoplatonism[19]

The thought of Plotinus was influenced by the writings of Plato, his eclectic study of the various school traditions, and his own personal insight and philosophical reasonings. While it is not possible to adequately treat the intricacies and range of Neoplatonic thought in the space available, it would at least be useful here to point out several general observations which are characteristic of Neoplatonic thought from Plotinus onwards:

1) There exist a plurality of spheres of being, hierarchically arranged in descending order, forming a series proceeding from higher to lower degrees of being with the last, lowest, and most unreal sphere of being comprising the universe which exists in time and space and is perceptible to the senses.

2) Each sphere of being is derived from its superior. While likened to 'emanation', this derivation is not a process which occurs in time or space, and the relation is one of logical implication rather than spatio-temporal or efficient causality.

3) Each derived being is established in its own reality by a turning back towards its superior in a movement of contemplative desire; hence the Neoplatonic universe is characterized by a double movement of outgoing and return.

4) Each sphere of being is an image or expression on a lower level of the sphere above it.

5) Degrees of being are also degrees of unity; hence, in each subsequent sphere of being there is greater multiplicity, more separateness, and increasing limitation— until the minimal unity of the spatio-temporal world is reached.

6) The supreme sphere of being, which might be characterized as pure Intelligence, is itself derived from a principle which, as the *source* of being, cannot in itself be described *as* being—it is *above being* and therefore fully indeterminate. This is not the indeterminateness of a most universal concept, but an ontic indeterminateness, i.e. fullest being precisely because it is not limited to being this or that.

7) Insofar as this ultimate principle has no determinations, attributes or limitations it cannot really be named, but for the sake of convenience it may be referred to as "the One" owing to its ultimate simplicity. It may also be called "the Good" since it is the source of all perfection and the ultimate goal of return.

8) Man's knowledge of this supreme principle, since it is devoid of any specific traits, must be radically different from the knowledge of any other object since no predicates may be applied to it. Hence, it can only be known if the mind is raised to an immediate union with it, a union which cannot be imagined or described.

The Mystical Ascent

It was Socrates who first stated the idea that "philosophy is a practice of death,"[20] and the mystical ascent of the Neoplatonists such as Porphyry is a form of death in itself, for it is through dying to the distractions of the senses that the higher life of the intelligible sphere is discovered. By dying to the senses, "the rushing stream of outward things,"[21] the philosopher moves toward identification with the omnipresent higher strata of his being which has been obscured by his immersion in the confusion and multiplicity of the external world. Hence, the mystical 'ascent' does not occur in space any more than emanation occurs in time; rather, it is, to paraphrase Plotinus, "an awakening to a new way of seeing which all men possess but which few men use."

Porphyry writes "The soul binds herself to the body by a conversion toward the affections experienced by the body. She detaches herself from the body by 'apathy,' turning away from the body's affections."[22] By dying to the lower, man discovers the life of the higher. Concerning this death Porphyry observes in the *Launching-Points to the Realm of Mind* that "There is a double death. One, known by all men, consists in the separation of the body with the soul; the other, characteristic of philosophers, results in the separation of the soul from the body."[23]

How, then, is this dying to the world of Becoming and awakening to the life of Being accomplished? It is through self-knowledge and the subsequent purification of the soul through the operation of the virtues, which Porphyry groups into a hierarchy of four types: the civil, purificatory, contemplative and exemplary. As he notes, "There is a difference between the virtues of the citizen, those of the man who rises to contemplation, and who, on this account, is said to possess a contemplative mind; those of him who contemplates intelligence; and finally those of pure Intelligence, which is completely separated from the soul."[24]

This scale or ladder of virtues Porphyry is developing from the ethical thought of Plotinus, yet both are relying on the hierarchy of knowledge and being articulated by Plato in the *Republic*, in connection with the famous allegory of the cave.[25] In the well-known passage the story is told of a group of prisoners who, since birth, have been confined in a cave, and so restrained that they can only face a particular wall. However, above in the opposite direction, there is an opening in the cave to the upper world from whence enters the light of day. In the upper world people are moving objects around and the shadows of this activity are falling upon the wall of the cave. These shadows the prisoners see and take to be reality, unaware of their higher source.

Such, Plato states, is the typical situation of humanity. The realm of the cave corresponds to the World of Appearances and Becoming (this world being dominated by mere assumption and human opinion); the realm above, the source of light, is the World of Reality and Being. According to the Platonic tradition, the world of authentic Being comprehends within itself all those principles and causes of which the world of phenomenal shadows is an effect, a mere after-image as it were.

In explaining this allegory, Plato states in a forthright fashion that "The ascent to see things in the upper world you may take as standing for the upward journey of the soul into the region of the intelligible."[26]

Plato in the *Republic* spells out the path of ascent from the world of appearances to the world of the real and also describes the educational process through which the soul's perceptions may pass upwards from the world of image and opinion to that of rational thought, and from rational thought to the direct knowledge of universal Forms or Ideas.[27] It is to these four levels of cognition and being that Porphyry's virtues correspond, and he teaches that each of the cardinal virtues (i.e., wisdom, courage, temperance and justice) exists and operates on each level of being in a slightly altered hierarchical fashion. Thus, Porphyry in *The Launching-Points to the Realm of Mind* demonstrates the relationship which exists between metaphysics or ontology (the levels of being), epistemology (the levels of knowledge), and ethics (the ideal way of life on each level of being and knowing):

> The object of the civil virtues is to moderate our passions so as to conform our conduct to the laws of human nature. That of the purificatory virtues is to detach the soul completely from the passions. That of the contemplative virtues is to apply the soul to intellectual operations, even

to the extent of no longer having to think of the need of freeing oneself from the passions. Last, that of the exemplary virtues is similar to that of the other virtues. Thus the practical virtues make man virtuous; the purificatory virtues make man divine, or make of the good man a protecting deity; the contemplative virtues deify; while the exemplary virtues make a man the parent of divinities.[28]

The beginning of the philosophical ascent occurs in realizing the illusory aspects of the world, when the phenomenal world is considered in respect to the intelligible principles of which it is a reflection. In his letter, Porphyry asks Marcella "What was it then that we learnt from those men who possess the clearest knowledge to be found among mortals? Was it not this—that I am in reality not this person who can be touched or perceived by any of the senses, but that which is farthest removed from the body, the colourless and formless essence which can by no means be touched by hands, but is grasped by the mind alone?"[29]

To the Neoplatonist, the soul is a perfect essence when turned to those things above, an intellect when conformed to Intelligence. As such, its relation to the body is of an *a priori* nature; the body is related to the soul, in a dynamic fashion, as an effect is related to a cause. In the same way the nature of being is of a hierarchical nature, so too is the nature of the person. A Platonist would argue that a person's true essence so far transcends the nature of the body as to make any other conclusion, in reality, the most unfortunate of self-deceptions. The life of the body, nonetheless, is a reflection of the life of the

soul on the lowest level. This realization, that the body
is an effect of the soul and not vice versa, is the necessary
starting point of the divine ascent, the path toward diviniza-
tion; as Porphyry notes in the *Launching-Points*, "To begin
with, the foundation of purification is to know oneself,
to realize that he is a soul bound to a foreign being, of
a different nature."[30] Likewise, Porphyry observes in the
Letter to Marcella that "Unless you consider that your
body is joined to you as the outer covering to the child
in the womb and the stalk to the sprouting corn, you
cannot know yourself. Nor can anyone know himself who
does not hold this opinion. As the outer covering grows
with the child, and the stalk with the corn, yet, when
they come to maturity, both are cast away, thus too the
body which is fastened to the soul at birth is not a part
of the man. But as the outer covering was formed with
the child that it may come to being in the womb, so
likewise the body was yoked to the man that he may
come to being on earth. In as far as a man turns toward
the mortal part of himself, in so far he makes his mind
incommensurate with immortality. And in as far as he
refrains from sharing the feelings of the body, in such
a measure does he approach the divine."[31]

With this realization in mind, "when one is convinced
of this truth, one should gather oneself together within
himself, detaching himself from the body, and freeing
himself entirely from the passions."[32] This passage from
the *Launching-Points* about 'gathering oneself together'
strongly parallels the remarkable section in the *Letter* where
Porphyry remarks that, even though he is absent, Marcella
would meet with him "in all purity...if you would practise

to ascend into yourself, collecting together all the powers which the body has scattered and broken up into a multitude of parts unlike their former unity to which concentration lent strength."[33]

While Porphyry's attitude is ascetical, one must not assume that the Neoplatonists took a negative view of the material world, nor, for that matter, of the body. The universe is one life, stretching from the highest to the lowest. The physical world is, in fact, the image of Soul, Soul is a reflection of Intelligence, and Intelligence is a reflection of the One. Even though utterly transcendent, a trace of the One is found on all levels of being. Matter is not *evil*; rather, "Matter is the lack of all existence; and consequently, what matter seems to be is a deception."[34] The phenomenal world may indeed consist of shadows flitting across the void of matter, but these shadows are the images of Soul, and Soul of the higher hypostases. The point where dualism enters the picture is in the individual soul's chosen orientation, whether her gaze be directed upward toward her Source and true Good, hence finding herself commensurate with immortality, or whether she looks downward in an attempt to further emesh herself in the web of non-being through the pursuit of vain and fleeting desires. Nonetheless, it must always be kept in mind that to all Neoplatonic philosophers the physical universe is the spatio-temporal theophany of the Divine *par excellence*: the cosmos is a living organism and the veritable image of God insofar as the divine may be approximated in time and space.

The Letter to Marcella

Porphyry's *Letter to Marcella* consists of two basic parts. The first part of the *Letter* addresses his wife Marcella, whom he has been forced to leave temporarily, and is also presumably addressed to the slanderers and critics who opposed the marriage, or who more probably used the marriage as an excuse to oppose Porphyry. Apparently Porphyry was accused of marrying Marcella for his own personal advantage, for money, sexual union, and because he needed someone to tend for him in his old age. Of course, Porphyry effectively counters these accusations, and from what we know of the philosopher it is difficult to believe that the accusations had any factual basis whatsoever—indeed, it is nearly impossible to imagine the seventy-year-old ascetic philosopher taking Marcella in wedlock in order to quench the raging fires of his sexual desire. We must assume that the facts are the way that Porphyry reports them—and wonder whether the marriage provided those individuals who didn't appreciate his anti-Christian polemics with an opportunity to oppose the august philosopher.

The second part of the letter is, quite appropriately, an ethical treatise in which is set out Porphyry's mildly ascetic moral philosophy. Here at times the presentation borders on the aphoristic, and it is known that Porphyry employed certain traditional sayings in its composition.[35] The entire letter is a brilliant piece of rhetoric—not rhetoric in the vulgar sense of mere persuasion without reference to ultimate reality, but rather the true rhetoric of philosophical exposition.[36] In his absence, Porphyry tells Marcella that her only true refuge is to be found in the

philosophical life. At one point he even refers obliquely
to the Platonic doctrine of recollection by noting that
his instruction has merely acted as a catalyst in helping
her to read the 'divine characters' latent within herself,
by helping her to 'remember' the universal knowledge
which eternally subsists within the soul but of which we
are generally unaware.[37]

Porphyry's *Letter*, as an ethical treatise, lacks the
metaphysical profundity of the *Launching-Points to the Realm
of Mind*. In fact, on the surface, no two works could appear more dissimilar. To understand the *Letter* no prior
knowledge of Neoplatonism is necessary; to understand
the *Launching-Points*, prior knowledge is helpful, to say
the least. But we have already pointed out several very
close similarities between these two books, and it takes
but little serious reflection to see that these apparently
dissimilar works are actually but two separate expressions
of one underlying, inclusive philosophy. In the *Launching-
Points* Porphyry expounds the metaphysical theory of in-
corporeals, the relation of the intelligible to the sensible,
and the hierarchy of virtues; in the *Letter to Marcella* he
shows how these principles relate to the everyday life of
the philosopher. Because one is a metaphysical treatise
and the other an ethical treatise they appear different;
but in the life of the philosopher they are inseparable.
The *Launching-Points*, admittedly, covers more ground than
the *Letter*, but the *Letter* is an introduction to the
purificatory or cathartic virtues, the acquisition of which
is prerequisite in the soul's assimilation to the higher intelligible realities, for as Porphyry observes in the *Launching-
Points*, "We should specially apply ourselves to purificatory

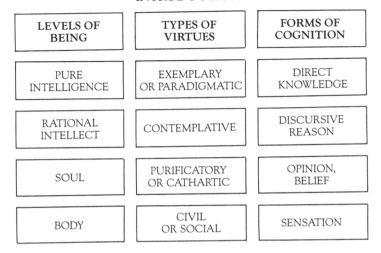

LEVELS OF BEING	TYPES OF VIRTUES	FORMS OF COGNITION
PURE INTELLIGENCE	EXEMPLARY OR PARADIGMATIC	DIRECT KNOWLEDGE
RATIONAL INTELLECT	CONTEMPLATIVE	DISCURSIVE REASON
SOUL	PURIFICATORY OR CATHARTIC	OPINION, BELIEF
BODY	CIVIL OR SOCIAL	SENSATION

The above chart illustrates the hierarchical relation which exists between the levels of being, types of virtues and forms of cognition in the thought of Porphyry the Neoplatonist.

virtues believing that we can acquire them even in this life; and that possession of them leads to superior virtues."[38]

For a full exposition of the different classes of virtues, to which we have already alluded, the reader is referred to the text of the *Launching-Points*. But we must briefly observe here how the four cardinal virtues of wisdom, courage, temperance and justice, according to Porphyry manifest different properties on different levels of being:

1) On the level of pure Mind or Intelligence the virtues are the exemplary or paradigmatic principles of eternal being itself, of the Intelligence which precedes even Soul. At this level, wisdom consists of Thought itself; courage is characterized by the identity, perseverance and concentration of intelligible essence; temperance is manifest in

the conversion of intellectual essence toward itself; and justice consists of the intellect's accomplishment of its characteristic function.

2) On the level of Discursive Intellect the object of the virtues is contemplative, the knowledge and science of true existence or reality. Here wisdom consists of contemplating the beings or principles contained by intelligence; courage consists of the steadfastness and impassibility by which the soul becomes assimilated to what she contemplates above; temperance consists of the conversion of the soul toward Intelligence; and justice consists of the soul fulfilling her characteristic function, that is to say directing her gaze toward Intelligence.

3) On the level of the animal Soul, the function of the virtues is purificatory or cathartic, their object being to raise the soul to genuine existence.

4) Finally, at the level of Body or the sensible world, the function of the virtues is civic, and their object is to make us benevolent in our dealings with fellow human beings.

Through effort, the civil and purificatory virtues are attainable by many non-philosophers in this life. Indeed, the very integrity of society depends on the former. The higher virtues, the contemplative and exemplary, while ever-existent and potentially available to everyone, are usually only activated or acquired by those seriously involved in the philosophical life, that is to say those individuals who follow the soul's turning back on the principle of Intellect or Being, which itself is forever both turning back and proceeding from the supreme principle 'beyond being' which is called the One.

Obviously, then, the civil and purificatory virtues represent the initial stage of the divine ascent. What does Porphyry have to say about the manifestation of the virtues on these levels of being?

The function of the civil virtues consists in the moderation of the passions to the point where one is able to follow the rational law of duty and live within the laws of human nature and human society. They are the most basic and necessary of virtues, and as such Porphyry does not even bother to define their characteristic operations in this sphere. We can be sure, however, that he followed the Platonic definitions of the *Republic*: in the social sphere, wisdom is good judgement about what is advantageous for society; courage is the preservation of the correct opinion about what is and what is not to be feared; temperance is the proper relation between the state and the polity, i.e., rule with consent of the governed; and justice is the harmony between the parts, where each part of society receives what it is due. These virtues hold true in smaller social groups and between individuals, functioning appropriately at different levels. In the *Letter to Marcella*, Porphyry does allude to the law of the state and interpersonal relations, and thus touches on the civil virtues. But in this work he is predominately concerned with the cathartic forms of virtue or excellence.

As we have observed, while the object of the civil virtues is to make us benevolent in our dealing with fellow human beings, the object of the cathartic virtues is to raise the soul to genuine existence. These virtues consist of detachment from things here below and direct man to abstain from activities in which the body predominates.

Through activation of the cathartic virtues the soul is led to look upward; it awakens to the knowledge of true existence and is hence assimilated to divinity. At this level of being, wisdom consists of not forming opinions in harmony with the body, but acting by oneself with pure thought; courage consists of not fearing separation from the passions of the body "as if death drove man into emptiness and annihilation";[39] temperance consists of not sharing in the passions of the body; while justice consists of obeying the principles of Reason and Intelligence as guides. While the end of the civil virtues is the moderation of passions, the end of the cathartic virtues is the obliteration of passions. It is to this end, and to the upward path of divine ascent, that Porphyry's *Letter to Marcella* is dedicated. And thus *Porphyry's Letter to His Wife Marcella* bears an intimate relation to the famous last words uttered by Plotinus—and recorded by his faithful student Porphyry, namely:

Try to bring back the god in you to the divine in the All.[40]

DAVID R. FIDELER

Notes

1) Eunapius, *Lives of the Philosophers*, 457.

2) Porphyry quoted by Eusebius, *History of the Church*, 6.19.

3) Eunapius, *Lives of the Philosophers*, 456.

4) Longinus, like Plotinus, had been a student of Ammonius of Alexandria, the great Platonist of whom little is known.

5) Eunapius, *Lives of the Philosophers*, 456.

6) Porphyry, *Life of Plotinus*, 18. (Armstrong translation.)

7) *Ibid.*, 15.

8) Porphyry the Phoenician, *Isagoge.* Toronto, Pontifical Institute of Medieval Studies, 1975. Translated by Edward W. Warren.

9) See Casey, P.M., "Porphyry and the Origin of the Book of Daniel," *Journal of Theological Studies*, N.S., XXVII, Pt. 1, 15-33.

10) Augustine, *City of God*, 19.23.

11) Plotinus, II.9.9.35-36.

12) This oracle, and the following ones, are quoted by Augustine in his *City of God*, Book 19, Chapter 23.

13) Dodds, E.R. *Pagan and Christian in an Age of Anxiety.* Cambridge, 1965, p. 109.

14) Wilken, R. *The Christians as the Romans Saw Them.* Yale, 1984, p. 160.

15) For the sources of these statements see Dodds, *Pagan and Christian in an Age of Anxiety*, p. 121.

16) *Letter to Marcella*, 24.

17) See Chapter 17, "Neoplatonic Faith," in Rist, J.M., *Plotinus: The Road to Reality*, Cambridge, 1967.

18) *Cambridge History of Later Greek and Early Medieval Philosophy*, p. 239.

19) This list of characteristics is based on that of Merlan, P., *From Platonism to Neoplatonism*, The Hague, Martinus Nijhoff, 1960, p. 1. Reference has also been made to the modified version of Armstrong.

20) *Phaedo*, 80E.

21) *Letter to Marcella*, 5.

22) *Launching-Points*, 9.

23) *Launching-Points*, 4. The *Launching-Points to the Realm of Mind*, as A.C. Lloyd observes, "is composed very largely of paraphrases of the *Enneads* arranged in paragraphs or 'propositions' whose exact order may here and

there be doubted. In fact it is a textbook of Plotinian Neoplatonism, although the belief that is is an easy introduction to the *Enneads* is unlikely to survive the experiment." (*Cambridge History of Later Greek and Early Medieval Philosophy*, p. 286.)

24) *Launching-Points*, 24.

25) *Republic*, 514A - 521B.

26) *Republic*, 517B.

27) Another very important Platonic passage on the philosophical ascent is the speech of Diotima, *Symposium* 201D - 212C.

28) *Launching-Points*, 1 (4).

29) *Letter to Marcella*, 8.

30) *Launching-Points*, 1 (4).

31) *Letter to Marcella*, 32.

32) *Launching-Points*, 1 (4).

33) *Letter to Marcella*, 10. Cf. *Phaedo*, 67C ff.

34) *Launching-Points*, 10.

35) These aphorisms bear an uncanny resemblance to those of a Christian collection, *The Sentences of Sextus*. This collection seems to be directly based on an earlier pagan collection, perhaps of Neopythagorean origin. For a list of parallels between the Christian edition, the aphorisms used by Porphyry, and a Pythagorean collection, see Chadwick, H., *The Sentences of Sextus*, Cambridge, 1959, chapter 4. For an English translation see *The Sentences of Sextus*, edited and translated by Edwards, R. and Wild, R., Chico, Scholars Press, 1981.

36) For a Platonic discussion of rhetoric see *Phaedrus*, 260 ff.

37) *Letter to Marcella*, 9.

38) *Launching-Points*, 1 (4).

39) *Launching-Points*, 1 (2).

40) Porphyry, *Life of Plotinus*, 2.

For further reading

Armstrong, A.H., editor. *The Cambridge History of Later Greek and Early Medieval Philosophy.* Cambridge, 1967.
—"Man in the Cosmos: A Study of Some Differences Between Pagan Neoplatonism and Christianity." In *Romanitas et Christianitas*, Amsterdam, North-Holland Publishing Company, 1973.

Bidez, J. *Vie de Porphyry.* Ghent-Leipzig, 1913.

Eunapius. "Lives of the Philosophers" in *Philostratus and Eunapius*, Harvard, Loeb Classical Library, 1921.

Plotinus. *The Enneads.* Translated by Armstrong, A.H. 6 vols. Harvard, Loeb Classical Library, 1966-.

Porphyry. *Launching-Points to the Realm of Mind.* Translated by Guthrie, K.S. Grand Rapids, Phanes Press, 1986.
—Porphyrios: *Pros Markellan.* Potscher, W., ed. and trans. Leiden, E.J. Brill, 1969. (A critical edition of the Greek text with a German translation and commentary.)

Rist, J.M. *Plotinus: The Road to Reality.* Cambridge, 1967.

Wilkin, R. *The Christians as the Romans Saw Them.* Yale, 1984.
—"Pagan Criticism of Christianity: Greek Religion and Christian Faith." In *Early Christian Literature and the Classical Intellectual Tradition.* Paris, Editions Beauchesne, 1979.

PORPHYRIOS
ΠΡΟΣ ΜΑΡΚΕΛΛΑΝ

PORPHYRY TO MARCELLA

I CHOSE YOU as my wife, Marcella, though you were the mother of five daughters and two sons, some of whom are still little children, and the others approaching a marriageable age; and I was not deterred by the multitude of things which would be needful for their maintenance. And it was not for the sake of having children that I wedded you, deeming that the lovers of true wisdom were my children, and that your children too would be mine if ever these should embrace right philosophy, when educated by us. Nor yet was it because a superfluity of riches had fallen either to your lot or mine. For such necessaries as are ours must suffice us who are poor. Neither did I expect that you would afford me any ease through your ministrations as I advanced in years, for your frame is delicate, and more in need of care from others than fitted to succour or watch over them. Nor yet did I desire other housewifely care from you, nor sought I after honour and praise from those who would not willingly have undertaken such a burden for the mere sake of doing good. Nay, it was far otherwise, for through the folly of your fellow-citizens, and their envy toward you and yours, I encountered much ill-speaking, and contrary to all expectation, I fell into danger of death at their hands on your behalf.

2. For none of these causes did I choose another to be partner of my life, but there was a twofold and reasonable cause that swayed me. One part was that I deemed I should thus propitiate the gods of generation; just as Socrates in his prison chose to compose popular music, for the sake of safety in his departure from life, instead of his customary labours in philosophy, so did I strive to propitiate the divinities who preside over this tragi-comedy of ours, and shrank not from celebrating in all willingness the marriage hymn, though I took as my lot your numerous children, and your straitened circumstances, and the malice of evil-speakers. Nor were there lacking any of those passions usually connected with a play—jealousy, hatred, laughter, quarrelling and anger; this alone excepted, that it was not with a view to ourselves but for the sake of others that we enacted this spectacle in honour of the gods.

3. Another worthier reason, in nowise resembling that commonplace one, was that I admired you because your disposition was suited to true philosophy; and when you were bereaved of your husband, a man dear to me, I deemed it not fitting to leave you without a helpmeet and wise protector suited to your character. Wherefore I drove away all who were minded to use insult under false pretence, and I endured foolish contumely, and bore in patience with the plots laid against me, and strove, as far as in my power lay, to deliver you from all who tried to lord it over you. I recalled you also to your proper mode of life, and gave you a share in philosophy, pointing

out to you a doctrine that should guide your life. And who could be a more faithful witness to me than yourself, for I should deem it shame to equivocate to you, or conceal aught of mine from you, or to withhold from you (who honours truth above all things, and therefore did deem our marriage a gift of Heaven) a truthful relation from beginning to end of all that I have done with respect to and during our union.

4. Now had my business permitted me to remain longer in your country, it would have been possible for you to still your thirst with fresh and plentiful draughts from fountains close at hand, so that, not contenting yourself with as much of this gift as would be requisite for ends of utility, you could rejoice in easily supplying yourself at your leisure with plentiful refreshment. But now the affairs of the Greeks requiring me, and the gods too urging me on, it was impossible for you, though willing, to answer the summons, with so large a number of daughters attending you. And I held it to be both foolish and wicked to cast them thus without you among ill-disposed men. And now that I am compelled to delay here, though I cherish the hope of a speedy return, I would deem it right to warn you to keep firm hold of those gifts you did receive in those ten months during which you did live with me, and not to cast away that you already have from desire and longing for more. As for me, I am making what haste I can to rejoin you.

5. Yet considering the uncertainty of the future, in traveling I must, in sending you consolation, lay upon you commands. And I would say somewhat that this is more suitable for you than to take care of yourself and your

house,

And keep all things in safety,

left behind as you are, not unlike Philoktetes in the tragedy, suffering from his sore, though his sore was caused by a baleful serpent, yours by the knowledge of the nature and extent of the descent to earth which has befallen our souls. Albeit the gods have not forsaken us, as the sons of Atreus forsook him, but they have become our helpers and have been mindful of us. Now seeing you are hard beset in a contest, attended with much wrestling and labour, I earnestly beg you to keep firm hold upon philosophy, the only sure refuge, and not to yield more than is fitting to the perplexities caused by my absence. Do not from desire for my instruction cast away what you have already received, and do not faint before the multitude of other cares that encompass you, abandoning yourself to the rushing stream of outward things. Rather bear in mind that it is not by ease that men attain the possession of the true good, and practise yourself for the life you expect to lead by help of those very troubles which are the only opponents to your fortitude that are able to disturb and constrain you. As for plots laid against us, it is easy for those to despise them who are accustomed to disregard all that does not lie in our own power, and who deem that injustice rather recoils upon the doer than injures those who believe that the worst injury inflicted on them can cause them but little loss.

6. Now you may console yourself for the absence of him who sustains your soul, and is to you father, husband, teacher, and kindred, yea, if you will, even fatherland,

though this seems to offer a reasonable ground for unhappiness, by placing before yourself as arbiter not feeling but reason. In the first place consider that, as I have said before, it is impossible that those who desire to be mindful of their return, should accomplish their journey home from this terrestrial exile pleasantly and easily, as through some smooth plain. For no two things can be more entirely opposed to one another than a life of pleasure and ease, and the ascent to the gods. As the summits of mountains cannot be reached without danger and toil, so it is not possible to emerge from the inmost depths of the body through pleasure and ease which drag men down to the body. For 'tis by anxious thought that we reach the road, and by recollection of our fall. But even if we encounter difficulties in our way, hardship is natural to the ascent, for it is given to the gods alone to lead an easy life. But ease is most dangerous for souls which have sunk to this earthly life, making them forgetful in the pursuit of alien things, and bringing on a state of slumber if we fall asleep, beguiled by alluring visions.

7. Now there are some chains that are of very heavy gold, but, because of their beauty, they persuaded women who in their folly do not perceive the weight, that they contribute to ornament, and thus got them to bear fetters easily. But other fetters which are of iron compelled them to a knowledge of their sins, and by pain forced them to repent and seek release from the weight; while escape from the golden imprisonment, through the delight felt in it, often causes grievous woe. Whence it has seemed to men of wisdom that labours conduce to virtue more than do pleasures. And to toil is better for man, aye, and

for woman too, than to let the soul be puffed up and ener-
vated by pleasure. For labour must lead the way to every
fair possession, and he must toil who is eager to attain
virtue. You know that Heracles and the Discouri, and
Asclepius and all other children of the gods, through toil
and steadfastness accomplished the blessed journed to
heaven. For it is not those who live a life of pleasure that
make the ascent to the gods, but rather those who have
nobly learnt to endure the greatest misfortunes.

8. I know full well that there could be no greater contest than that which now lies before you, since you think
that in me you will lose the path of safety and the guide
therein. Yet your circumstances are not altogether unen-
durable, if you cast from yourself the unreasoning distress
of mind which springs from the feelings, and deem it no
trivial matter to remember those words by which you were
with divine rites initiated into true philosophy, approving
by your deeds the fidelity with which they have been
apprehended. For it is a man's actions that naturally afford demonstrations of his opinions, and whoever holds
a belief must live in accordance with it, in order that
he may himself be a faithful witness to the hearers of
his words. What was it then that we learnt from those
men who possess the clearest knowledge to be found among
mortals? Was it not this—that I am in reality not this
person who can be touched or perceived by any of the
senses, but that which is farthest removed from the body,
the colourless and formless essence which can by no
means be touched by the hands, but is grasped by the
mind alone. And it is not from outward things that we
receive those principles which are implanted in us. We

receive only the keynote as in a chorus, which recalls to our remembrance those things which we received from the god who gave them us ere we set forth on our wanderings.

9. Moreover, is not every emotion of the soul most hostile to its safety? And is not want of education the mother of all the passions? Now education does not consist in the absorption of a large amount of knowledge, but in casting off the affections of the soul. Now the passions are the beginning of diseases. And vice is the disease of the soul; and every vice is disgraceful. And the disgraceful is opposed to the good. Now since the divine nature is good, it is impossible for it to consort with vice, since Plato says it is unlawful for the impure to approach the pure. Wherefore even now we need to purge away all our passions, and the sins that spring therefrom. Was it not this you did so much approve, reading as it were divine characters within yourself, disclosed by my words? Is it not then absurd, though you are persuaded that you have in yourself the saving and the saved, the losing and the lost, wealth and poverty, father and husband, and a guide to all true good, to pant after the mere shadow of a leader, as though you had not within yourself a true leader, and all riches within your own power? And this must you lose and fly from, if you descend to the flesh, instead of turning towards that which saves and is saved.

10. As for my shadow and visible image, as you were not profited by their presence, so now their absence is not hurtful if you attempt to fly from the body. But you would meet me in all purity, and I should be most truly present and associated with you, night and day, in purity

and with the fairest kind of converse which can never be broken up, if you would practise to ascend into yourself, collecting together all the powers which the body has scattered and broken up into a multitude of parts unlike their former unity to which concentration lent strength. You should collect and combine into one the thoughts implanted within you, endeavouring to isolate those that are confused, and to drag to light those that are enveloped in darkness. The divine Plato too made this his starting-point, summoning us away from the sensible to the intelligible. Also if you would remember, you would combine what you have heard, and recall it by memory, desiring to turn your mind to discourses of this kind as to excellent counsellors, and afterwards practising in action what you have learned, bearing it in mind in your labours.

11. Reason tells us that the divine is present everywhere and in all men, but that only the mind of the wise man is sanctified as its temple, and God is best honoured by him who knows Him best. And this must naturally be the wise man alone, who in wisdom must honour the Divine, and in wisdom adorn for it a temple in his thought, honouring it with a living statue, the mind moulded in His image . . . . Now God is not in need of any one, and the wise man is in need of God alone. For no one could become good and noble, unless he knew the goodness and beauty which proceed from the Deity. Nor is any man unhappy, unless he has fitted up his soul as a dwelling-place for evil spirits. To the wise man God gives the authority of a god. And a man is purified by the knowledge of God, and issuing from God, he follows after righteousness.

12. Let God be at hand to behold and examine every act and deed and word. And let us consider Him the author of all our good deeds. But of evil we ourselves are the authors, since it is we who made choice of it, but God is without blame. Wherefore we should pray to God for that which is worthy of Him, and we should pray for what we could attain from none other. And we must pray that we may attain after our labours those things that are preceded by toil and virtue; for the prayer of the slothful is but vain speech. Neither ask of God what you will not hold fast when you have attained it, since God's gifts cannot be taken from you, and He will not give what you will not hold fast. What you will not require when you are rid of the body, that despise, but practise yourself in that you will need when you are set free, calling on God to be your helper. You will need none of those things which chance often gives and again takes away. Do not make any request before the fitting season, but only when God makes plain the right desire implanted by nature within you.

13. Hereby can God best be reflected, who cannot be seen by the body, nor yet by an impure soul darkened by vice. For purity is God's beauty, and His light is the life-giving flame of truth. Every vice is deceived by ignorance, and turned astray by wickedness. Wherefore desire and ask of God what is in accordance with His own will and nature, well assured that, inasmuch as a man longs after the body and the things of the body in so far does he fail to know God, and is blind to the sight of God, even though all men should hold him as a god. Now the wise man, if known by only few, or, if you will,

unknown to all, yet is known by God, and is reflected by his likeness to Him. Let then your mind follow after God, and let the soul follow the mind, and let the body be subservient to the soul as far as may be, the pure body serving the pure soul. For if it be defiled by the emotions of the soul, the defilement reacts upon the soul itself.

14. In a pure body where soul and mind are loved by God, words should conform with deeds: since it is better for you to cast a stone at random than a word, and to be defeated speaking the truth rather than conquer through deceit; for he who conquers by deceit is worsted in his character. And lies are witnesses unto evil deeds. It is impossible for a man who loves God also to love pleasure and the body, for he who loves these must needs be a lover of riches. And he who loves riches must be unrighteous. And the unrighteous man is impious towards God and his fathers, and transgresses against all men. And though he slay whole hecatombs in sacrifice, and adorn the temples with ten thousand gifts, yet is he impious and godless, and at heart a plunderer of holy places. Wherefore we should shun all addicted to love of the body as godless and impure.

15. Do not associate with any one whose opinions cannot profit you, nor join with him in converse about God. For it is not safe to speak of God with those who are corrupted by false opinion. Yea, and in their presence to speak truth or falsehood about God is fraught with equal danger. It is not fitting for a man who is not purified from unholy deeds to speak of God himself, nor must we suppose that he who speaks of Him with such is not guilty of a crime. We should hear and use speech concern-

ing God as though in His presence. Godlike deeds should precede talk of God, and in the presence of the multitude we should keep silence concerning Him, for the knowledge of God is not suitable to the vain conceit of the soul. Esteem it better to keep silence than to let fall random words about God. You will become worthy of God if you deem it wrong either to speak or do or know aught unworthy of Him. Now a man who was worthy of God would be himself a god.

16. You will best honour God by making your mind like unto Him, and this you can do by virtue alone. For only virtue can draw the soul upward to that which is akin to it. Next to God there is nothing great but virtue, yet God is greater than virtue. Now God strengthens the man who does noble deeds. But an evil spirit is the instigator of evil deeds. The wicked soul flies from God, and would fain that His providence did not exist, and it shrinks from the divine law which punishes all the wicked. But the wise man's soul is like God, and ever beholds Him and dwells with Him. If the ruler takes pleasure in the ruled, then God too cares for the wise man and watches over him. Therefore is the wise man blest, because he is in God's keeping. 'Tis not his speech that is acceptable to God, but his deed; for the wise man honours God even in his silence, while the fool dishonours Him even while praying and offering sacrifice. Thus the wise man only is a priest; he only is beloved by God, and knows how to pray.

17. The man who practises wisdom practises the knowledge of God; and he shows his piety not by continued prayers and sacrifices but by his actions. No one

could become well-pleasing to God by the opinions of men or the vain talk of the Sophists. But he makes himself well-pleasing and consecrated to God by assimilating his own disposition to the blessed and incorruptible nature. And it is he who makes himself impious and displeasing to God, for God does not injure him (since the divine nature can only work good), but he injures himself, chief-ly through his wrong opinion concerning God. Not he who disregards the images of the gods is impious, but he who holds the opinions of the multitude concerning God. But do you entertain no thought unworthy of God or of His blessedness and immortality.

18. The chief fruit of piety is to honour God according to the laws of our country, not deeming that God has need of anything, but that He calls us to honour Him by His truly reverend and blessed majesty. We are not harmed by reverencing God's altars, nor benefited by neglecting them. But whoever honours God under the impression that He is in need of him, he unconsciously deems himself greater than God. 'Tis not when they are angry that the gods do us harm, but when they are not understood. Anger is foreign to the gods, for anger is involuntary, and there is nothing involuntary in God. Do not then dishonour the divine nature by false human opinions, since you will not injure the eternally blessed One, whose immortal nature is incapable of injury, but you will blind yourself to the conception of what is great and chiefest.

19. Again you could not suppose my meaning to be this when I exhort you to reverence the gods, since it would be absurd to command this as though the matter

admitted a question. And we do not worship Him only by doing or thinking this or that, neither can tears or supplications turn God from His purpose, nor yet is God honoured by sacrifices nor glorified by plentiful offerings; but it is the godlike mind that remains stably fixed in its place that is united to God. For like must needs approach like. But the sacrifices of fools are mere food for fire, and the offerings they bring help the robbers of temples to lead their evil life. But, as was said before, let your temple be the mind that is within you. This must you tend and adorn, that it may be a fitting dwelling for God. Yet let not the adornment and the reception of God be but for a day, to be followed by mockery and folly and the return of the evil spirit.

20. If, then, you ever bear in mind that wheresoever your soul walks and inspires your body with activity, God is present and overlooks all your counsels and actions, then will you feel reverence before the unbegotten presence of the spectator, and you will have God to dwell with you. And even though your mouth discourse the sound of some other thing, let your thought and mind be turned towards God. Thus shall even your speech be inspired, shining through the light of God's truth and flowing the more easily; for the knowledge of God makes discourse short.

21. But wheresoever forgetfulness of God shall enter in, there must the evil spirit dwell. For the soul is a dwelling-place, as you have learned, either of gods or of evil spirits. If the gods are present, it will do what is good both in word and in deed; but if it has welcomed in the evil guest, it does all things in wickedness. Whensoever, then, you

behold a man doing or rejoicing in that which is evil, know that he has denied God in his heart and is the dwelling-place of an evil spirit. They who believe that God exists and governs all things have this reward of their knowledge and firm faith: they have learnt that God has forethought for all things, and that there exist angels, divine and good spirits, who behold all that is done, and from whose notice we cannot escape. Being persuaded that this is so, they are careful not to fall in their life, keeping before their eyes the constant presence of the gods whence they cannot escape. And they have attained to a wise mode of life, and know the gods and are known by them.

22. On the other hand, they who believe that the gods do not exist and that the universe is not governed by God's providence, have this punishment: they neither believe themselves, nor yet do they put faith in others who assert that the gods exist, but think that the universe is directed by a whirling motion void of reason. Thus they have cast themselves into unspeakable peril, trusting to an unreasoning and uncertain impulse in the events of life; and they do all that is unlawful in the endeavour to remove the belief in God. Assuredly such men are forsaken by the gods for their ignorance and unbelief. Yet they cannot flee and escape the notice of the gods or of justice their attendant, but having chosen an evil and erring life, though they know not the gods, yet are they known by them and by justice that dwells with the gods.

23. Even if they think they honour the gods, and are persuaded that they exist, yet neglect virtue and wisdom, they really have denied the divinities and dishonour them.

Mere unreasoning faith without right living does not attain to God. Nor is it an act of piety to honour God without having first ascertained in what manner He delights to be honoured. If, then, He is gratified and won over by libations and sacrifices, it would not be just that while all men make the same requests they should obtain different answers to their prayers. But if there is nothing that God desires less than this, while he delights only in the purifications of the mind, which every man can attain of his own free choice, what injustice could there be? But if the divine nature delights in both kinds of service, it should receive honour by sacred rites according to each man's power, and by the thoughts of his mind even beyond that power. It is not wrong to pray to God, since ingratitude is a grievous wrong.

24. No god is in fault for a man's wickedness, but the man who has chosen it for himself. The prayer which is accompanied by base actions is impure, and therefore not acceptable to God; but that which is accompanied by noble actions is pure, and at the same time acceptable.

There are four first principles that must be upheld concerning God—faith, truth, love, hope. We must have faith that our only salvation is in turning to God. And having faith, we must strive with all our might to know the truth about God. And when we know this, we must love Him we do know. And when we love Him we must nourish our souls on good hopes for our life, for it is by their good hopes good men are superior to bad ones. Let then these four principles be firmly held.

25. Next let these three laws be distinguished. First, the law of God; second, the law of human nature; third,

that which is laid down for nations and states. The law of nature fixes the limits of bodily needs, and shows what is necessary to these, and condemns all striving after which is needless and superfluous. Now that which is established and laid down for States regulates by fixed agreements the common relations of men, by their mutual observance of the covenants laid down. But the divine law is implanted by the mind, for their welfare, in the thoughts of reasoning souls, and it is found truthfully inscribed therein. The law of humanity is transgressed by him who through vain opinions know it not, owing to his excessive love for the pleasures of the body. But the conventional law is subject to expediency, and is differently laid down at different times according to the arbitrary will of the prevailing government. It punishes him who transgresses it, but it cannot reach a man's secret thoughts and intentions.

26. The divine law is unknown to the soul that folly and intemperance have rendered impure, but it shines forth in self-control and wisdom. It is impossible to transgress this, for there is nothing in man that can transcend it. Nor can it be despised, for it cannot shine forth in a man who will despise it. Nor is it moved by chances of fortune, because it is in truth superior to chance and stronger than any form of violence. Mind alone knows it, and diligently pursues the search thereafter, and finds it imprinted in itself, and supplies from it food to the soul as to its own body. We must regard the rational soul as the body of the mind, which the mind nourishes by bringing into recognition, through the light that is in it, the thoughts within, which mind imprinted and engrav-

ed in the soul in accordance with the truth of the divine law. Thus mind is become teacher and saviour, nurse, guardian and leader, speaking the truth in silence, unfolding and giving forth the divine law; and looking on the impressions thereof in itself it beholds them implanted in the soul from all eternity.

27. You must therefore first understand the law of nature, and then proceed to the divine law, by which also the natural law has been prescribed. And if you make these your starting-point you shall never fear the written law. For written laws are made for the benefit of good men, not that they may do no wrong, but that they may not suffer it. Natural wealth is limited, and it is easy to attain. But the wealth desired of vain opinions has no limits, and is hard to attain. The true philosopher therefore, following nature and not vain opinions, is self-sufficing in all things; for in the light of the requirements of nature every possession is some wealth, but in the light of unlimited desires even the greatest wealth is but poverty. Truly it is no uncommon thing to find a man who is rich if tried by the standard of vain opinions. No fool is satisfied with what he possesses; he rather mourns for what he has not. Just as men in a fever are always thirsty through the grievous nature of their malady, and desire things quite opposed to one another, so men whose souls are ill-regulated are ever in want of all things, and experience ever-varying desires through their greed.

28. Wherefore the gods, too, have commanded us to purify ourselves by abstaining from food and from love, bringing those who follow after piety within the law of that nature which they themselves have formed, since

everything which transgresses this law is loathsome and deadly. The multitude, however, fearing simplicity in their mode of life, because of this fear, turn to the pursuits that can best procure riches. And many have attained wealth, and yet not found release from their troubles, but have exchanged them for greater ones. Wherefore philosophers say that nothing is so necessary as to know thoroughly what is unnecessary, and moreover that to be self-sufficing is the greatest of all wealth, and that it is honourable not to ask anything of any man. Wherefore, too, they exhort us to strive, not to acquire some necessary thing, but rather to remain of good cheer if we have not acquired it.

29. Neither let us accuse our flesh as the cause of great evils, nor attribute our troubles to outward things. Rather let us seek the cause of these things in our souls, and casting away every vain striving and hope for fleeting joys, let us become completely masters of ourselves. For a man is unhappy either through fear or through unlimited and empty desire. Yet if he bridle these, he can attain to a happy mind. But in as far as you are in want, it is through forgetfulness of your nature that you feel the want. For hereby you cause to yourself vague fears and desires. And it were better for you to be content and lie on a bed of rushes than to be troubled though you have a golden couch and a luxurious table acquired by labour and sorrow. Whilst the pile of wealth is growing bigger, life is growing wretched.

30. Do not think it unnatural that when the flesh cries out for anything, the soul should cry out too. The cry of the flesh is, "Let me not hunger, or thirst, or shiver,"

and 'tis hard for the soul to restrain these desires. 'Tis hard, too, for it by help of its own natural self-sufficing to disregard day by day the exhortations of nature, and to teach it to esteem the concerns of life as of little account. And when we enjoy good fortune, to learn to bear ill fortune, and when we are unfortunate not to hold of great account the possessions of those who enjoy good fortune. And to receive with a calm mind the good gifts of fortune, and to stand firm against her seeming ills. Yea, all that the many hold good is but a fleeting thing.

31. But wisdom and knowledge have no part in chance. It is not painful to lack the gifts of chance, but rather to endure the unprofitable trouble of vain ambition. For every disturbance and unprofitable desire is removed by the love of true philosophy. Vain is the word of that philosopher who can ease no mortal trouble. As there is no profit in the physician's art unless it cure the diseases of the body, so there is none in philosophy, unless it expel the troubles of the soul. These and other like commands are laid on us by the law of our nature.

32. Now the divine law cries aloud in the pure region of the mind: "Unless you consider that your body is joined to you as the outer covering to the child in the womb and the stalk to the sprouting corn, you can not know yourself." Nor can anyone know himself who does not hold this opinion. As the outer covering grows with the child, and the stalk with the corn, yet, when they come to maturity, both are cast away, thus too the body which is fastened to the soul at birth is not a part of the man. But as the outer covering was formed along with the child that it may come to being in the womb, so likewise the

body was yoked to the man that he may come to being
on the earth. In as far as a man turns to the mortal part
of himself, in so far he makes his mind incommensurate
with immortality. And in as far as he refrains from sharing the feelings of the body, in such a measure does he
approach the divine. The wise man who is beloved of
God strives and toils as much for the good of his soul
as others do for the good of their body. He deems that
he cannot become self-sufficing merely by remembering
what he has heard, but strives by practising it to hasten
on towards his duty.

33. Naked was he sent into the world, and naked shall
he call on Him that sent him. For God listens only to
those who are not weighed down by alien things, guard-
ing those who are pure from corruption. Consider it
a great help towards the blessed life if the captive in the
thralls of nature takes his captor captive. For we are bound
in the chains that nature has cast around us, by the belly,
the throat and the other parts of the body, and by the
use of these and the pleasant sensations that arise therefrom
and the fears they occasion. But if we rise superior to
their witchcraft, and avoid the snares laid by them, we
have led our captor captive. Neither trouble yourself much
whether you be male or female in body, nor look upon
yourself as a woman, for I did not approach you as such.
Flee all that is womanish in the soul, as though you had
a man's body about you. For what is born from a virgin
soul and a pure mind is most blessed, since imperishable
springs from imperishable. But what the body produces
is held corrupt by all the gods.

34. It is a great proof of wisdom to hold the body in

thrall. Often men cast off certain parts of the body; be ready for the soul's safety to cast away the whole body. Hesitate not to die for whose sake you are willing to live. Let reason then direct all our impulses, and banish from us tyrannous and godless masters. For the rule of the passions is harder than that of tyrants, since it is impossible for a man to be free who is governed by his passions. As many as are the passions of the soul, so many cruel masters have we.

35. Strive not to wrong your slaves nor to correct them when you are angry. And before correcting them, prove to them that you do this for their good, and give them an opportunity for excuse. When purchasing slaves, avoid the stubborn ones. Accustom yourself to do many things yourself, for our own labour is simple and easy. And men should use each limb for the purpose for which nature intended it to be used. Nature needs no more. They who do not use their own bodies, but make excessive use of others, commit a twofold wrong, and are ungrateful to nature that has given them these parts. Never use your bodily parts merely for the sake of pleasure, for it is far better to die than to obscure your soul by intemperance . . . . correct the vice of your nature . . . . If you give something to your slaves, distinguish the better ones by a share of honour . . . . for it is impossible that he who does wrong to men should honour God. But look on the love of mankind as the foundation of your piety. And . . . .

[HERE THE MS. ENDS ABRUPTLY.]

A Note Concerning
Phanes Press

PHANES PRESS *both publishes and distributes many fine books which relate to the traditional cosmology, philosophy and spirituality of the West. Some recently published and forthcoming titles include:*

The Secret Rose Garden of Shabistari
The Life of Proclus or Concerning Happiness
Porphyry's Launching-Points to the Realm of Mind
Porphyry: On the Cave of the Nymphs
The Pythagorean Sourcebook and Library
The Chaldean Oracles
Emperor Julian's Hymn to King Helios
Iamblichus's Exhortation to Philosophy

If you would like to obtain a copy of our illustrated catalogue, please write to:

PHANES PRESS
POST OFFICE BOX 6114
GRAND RAPIDS, MICHIGAN 49506
UNITED STATES OF AMERICA